GRIEF

A BASIC REACTION TO ALCOHOLISM

by
Joseph L. Kellermann

HAZELDEN
Center City, Minnesota 55012
1977

Third printing, November, 1979

ISBN: 0-89486-037-2
Printed in the United States of America

Depression or Grief?

"Grief is the real or the imaginary loss of a cherished person or thing. Depression, by contrast, exists despite all evidence to the contrary. The person suffering grief is very much aware of the nature of grief as to its cause or origin. The depressed person is not aware of the cause."

The above definition was given a few years ago by Dr. Hans Lowenbach, of the Duke University Medical Center, now retired. His essential contrast between grief and depression will be followed as well as his descriptions of the symptoms of grief and the suggested steps in recovery.

Depression is completely irrational and may be a psychotic condition. It does not respond to reason, intelligence, or to counseling, but in most cases is self-limiting. It may respond to medication or the treatment of a mental illness through chemotherapy.

Grief, on the other hand, is usually a normal loss reaction, but does not require the loss of a loved one by death. Any basic loss may produce grief, such as the damage to a new car or the loss of a family pet. Retirement and giving up responsibility may produce real grief. Losing a contract or a bid may induce grief. Teen-age lovers frequently experience grief, which is a part of growing up.

Separation or divorce brings grief even though both parties are aware that the action is necessary. Each loses something that was once very dear to them both.

The breaking away of a child as it passes through the period of adolescence may produce grief for a parent. If the parent tries to reach down and pull the child back, the grief increases. The parent must accept the child as a young adult who may or may not turn back to the parent. Pursuing the child in grief only makes it worse. Any family situation which focuses on the lost person or thing, rather than self, increases grief.

Grief is the universal experience of all persons of every race or creed. The only persons who escape grief are those who die before any human love is formed or experienced. Grief is common to all persons and it is included in the Beatitudes: "Blessed are those that mourn, for they shall be comforted." Mourning is working through grief, or the means whereby grief is overcome.

The only persons who are incapable of grief are those unable to experience love and affection with others. The capacity to love entails the experience of grief at some point in life. Husband or wife lose each other in time. Parent and child do the same. The experience of grief indicates the ability to care and relate to other persons. It also entails the ability to enjoy God's gifts to us, things in life which we cherish to the extent we miss them when lost.

Many counselors do not distinguish between depression and grief and treat them as one and the same thing. As the origin of each is entirely different, then working through each is an entirely different process. Unfortunately, in the field of alcoholism, grief is rarely mentioned in the literature and is not considered in most recovery programs for the alcoholic or family members. It is ignored, or even worse, grief-stricken persons are told that they are depressed, which is considered a form of mental illness.

As grief is a normal condition, medication is not indicated except for one specific purpose. At the time of death, it is permissible for the person who cannot sleep to have medication to get a good night's rest in order to go through the service of the burial of the dead and all that is entailed, which often requires facing an enormous number of persons.

If grief occurs, the grieving person must be permitted to experience grief and helped through grief with the most appropriate means available to the person. Each society and culture has its own process of working through grief, and persons must be permitted to do those things which they have been taught or think are proper in expressing their grief. The same is true in regards to expressions of grief which do not relate to death. The use of medication is an escape from the process of working through grief and postpones a return to a condition of normalcy which cannot occur until grief is resolved. To reduce the pain artificially is not an answer to grief.

Symptoms of Grief

The impact of grief on a person is clearly visible and manifests itself in several ways. The following are observable characteristics:

1. Fatigue and loss of energy are so pronounced that a grief-stricken person may collapse while walking across the floor. Grief drains off energy and the desire to be physically active.

2. Loss of appetite often occurs, although this is not true in all cases. Not eating, of course, adds to the loss of energy.

3. The face may look ten or fifteen years older. The curve of the mouth may turn down as a manifestation of sadness, the opposite of smiling, which often cannot be expressed. The whole countenance of the person takes on an appearance of sadness. This appearance may be only temporary or may last for weeks or months. Working through grief changes the facial expression to the extent that the facial expression is younger.

4. Initially, acute grief comes in waves, and much later on when grief has been overcome, a small wave of grief may appear for a moment. During an initial wave of grief, the person may think that he cannot breathe, and it may be so intense the person may feel he does not want to live. It is like being knocked down by an unexpected wave at the beach and having salt water get into the eyes, mouth, and nose and choke one. Wave after wave is to be expected, but the waves get smaller and the period of calm between the waves becomes longer and longer. In time the calm prevails, but the knowledge of this wave reaction of grief can be of great benefit to the grieving person, by permitting him to know the intensity will last a short while and a less painful condition will follow.

5. Another symptom of the grieving person that is in contrast with the depressed person is that the grieving person focuses on the lost object and can talk about nothing other than the person or thing that has been lost. In alcoholism, this is expressed by the constant focus on drinking and ignoring all other aspects of alcoholism, including any planning or realistic approach to the other problems involved. It does not reduce the grief of the family member (although it may relieve the tension of the moment), but leaves the person with increased emptiness. The constant verbalization about the grief object is a major symptom of grief as it relates to alcoholism.

6. Grief also entails such intense pain that it almost prevents the grieving person from doing anything which adds to pain at that time. This is why the grieving person benefits

enormously by working through grief if alcoholism is the source of grief. Until grief is overcome, it is virtually impossible to take creative action to cope with alcoholism more effectively. To do something which increases the intense pain of grief may seem impossible. Every person has a limit to the pain he can endure and acute grief for the moment is a bit more than most persons can bear if other pain is added at that time. When the grief dies down, the person will be able to consider beneficial action. At that moment, understanding, love, and comfort are needed, not advice.

So grief is the most normal and the most common of all human pains. It is not something that happens to other persons, it happens to all living persons who are capable of caring for others.

Grief of the Alcoholic

The nature of alcoholism produces losses for the alcoholic. There are several forms of alcoholism, but for the great majority of persons, it is a progressive illness which brings on greater losses as the person continues to drink over the years.

1. The first loss is the ability to drink in keeping with the social norm which involves the time, place, with whom, and how much. It also involves the conduct and responsibility of all involved in the social event. The first loss then, is the loss of interest in people and increased interest in the bottle.

2. The loss of memory of drinking experiences, which is alcoholic amnesia, commonly called a blackout. It appears in most in the late twenties, but may appear in the teens or at fifty, sixty, or even seventy in some rare cases. It is the first medical symptom of alcoholism that is clearly visible and occurs when

moderately intoxicated, and does not depend on overt drunkenness. This is a real loss of memory, not an imaginary one.

3. The loss of the ability to choose not to drink and stick with the choice. This ability is lost except in rare circumstances. This is a very real loss, but despite these losses and the accumulated problems resulting from drinking, the alcoholic goes back to the bottle again and again, which is the nature of the illness rather than the cause. Grief dissolves immediately in alcohol, as do all other problems for the moment.

4. The loss of the ability to maintain responsible social behavior when drinking. For many, the Jekyll to Hyde change in behavior is a characteristic of the illness. This is the mind-altering effect of alcohol on the alcoholic. One of the results of this loss of responsibility is the loss of the first job at a median age of thirty-seven years, which produces loss of income.

5. The loss of the ability to regain sobriety once intoxicated is termed addiction. It may appear much earlier, but usually appears as the alcoholic approaches or passes forty. The alcoholic has lost the ability to choose when to drink, how much to drink, and now the ability to sober up once intoxicated. It is devastating, but the alcoholic, either by compulsion or by determining that this loss is not real and can be overcome, turns back and back to the bottle.

6. The loss of the ability to support self and family due to the loss of physical health and chronic unemployment. Many alcoholics lose the ability to find employment in their late forties due to poor work records or simply the inability to stay sober long enough to find employment.

7. Finally, there is the loss of life in the early fifties, which is the median point of death for chronic alcoholics. There are alcoholics still drinking and even maintaining work activity in

the sixties, but there are others who die in their forties, including those who have the best medical and hospital care.

As self-idealization is often found in alcoholics, this series of losses, with increasing impact on the drinker, is devastating. These persons have tremendous desires to succeed, but there is an ever-widening gap between the idealization and their realization, which causes added grief and a sense of failure.

For the working alcoholic woman, the losses are much the same, but may occur over a shorter period of time.

For the housewife alcoholic, the same condition is true, other than the work record, which is more easily ignored or done by other family members. Losing a marriage at a much earlier date may be similar to loss of job for the employed male alcoholic. If anything, the sense of grief of the alcoholic wife is more painful than in the male.

Families Also Suffer Losses

Now for the losses of the family of the alcoholic, especially the spouse -- and for the sake of clarity, the following applies especially to the wife of an alcoholic. It is based largely on a study done by Joan K. Jackson some twenty-five years ago, *The Adjustments of the Family to the Crisis of Alcoholism.*

More recently, studies have been made which indicate that the spouse has a reaction to alcoholism that may be charted on a downward curve just as the progressive symptoms of the alcoholic. Recovery can also be charted in the same way; it is not instant, but is achieved over a period of time, which is also true for the alcoholic, as there are no instant cures for alcoholism.

As the losses of the alcoholic increase in severity, so does the grief of the spouse of the alcoholic increase, especially that of the wife. Initially she does not attempt to deal with the excessive drinking, because so many persons drink and excessive drinking is, unfortunately, all too acceptable in our culture, which increases the potential for alcoholism. So initial drunkenness does not bring grief in most families.

1. The first real grief appears when the wife attempts to keep the bottle away from the alcoholic, or keep him away from drinking situations or events. It simply does not work. The wife may stop going to social events where drinking is likely to occur, and she loses social contacts with other persons. Vacations cannot be planned in many cases, for drinking begins to disrupt the anticipated happiness of such events. So normal family living and normal social life are lost, which leads to sadness and grief.

2. The next noticeable loss is the loss of order. Life is chaos and confusion. Anything can happen, and usually does, in an alcoholic marriage, so plans cannot be made. The only real order is a state of disorder. This is a loss of responsibility within a home for all parties.

3. Most wives attempt to overcome this irresponsibility by taking over the responsibility as head of the house, and may even go to work to be certain that necessary bills are paid. This is a loss of proper role in marriage, as she becomes sole disciplinarian, dispenser of money and permission to do things, and is attempting to be both father and mother to the child. She also sees her children deprived of what others have in social life and benefits, and this adds to her grief.

4. A fourth loss for the wife may be described as attempts to escape from the reality of the situation. She may become a hermit, or become so active that she does not have time to

feel the losses. Having lost happiness in the home, she may attempt to find it everywhere other than in the family.

A common experience in this stage of adjustment of the family may be called "divorce within the home," which is just as grievous and damaging as separation. This condition may occur only while the alcoholic is drinking, or it may be a prolonged situation, but another tender part of a marriage has now disappeared.

5. Separation is something that happens in most alcoholic marriages, although it may be disguised in many ways. An extended visit with one's parents is a frequent example. Hospitalization for a psychosomatic illness is another. However, separation never occurs as frequently as threats, because the very idea of separation is too painful.

If separation occurs, the alcoholic usually stops drinking and asks that he be permitted to reenter the marriage based on promises not to drink again. Such a request is often granted without requiring that the alcoholic be engaged in a structured recovery program or active in Alcoholics Anonymous.

The wife usually reenters marriage without having become active in her own program to learn how to cope with alcoholism. The idea of divorce is painful and the separation so filled with emotional conflicts, most marriages are resumed after separation with no structured program for either husband or wife.

If reconciliation of the separation occurs without sufficient time and a recovery program for both, the end result is that drinking starts in a short period of time. The result is extreme grief for the wife, who feels that the painful process of separation did not work. She may feel utter despair and that it is a hopeless situation. The separation worked, in a sense, but it was the reconciliation which did not work, because neither was prepared for it. These are things a spouse should know before taking steps to separate.

Separation should never be undertaken in an effort to make the other party stop drinking. Separation may occur when to remain is so destructive it might take both parties beyond the point of no return. Separation may be undertaken if the sober spouse seeks help, enters a recovery program, and separates on the basis that the alcoholic chose not to enter a recovery program in order to solve the intolerable marriage problems. Separation should not be tried to force the alcoholic to stop drinking, but is justifiable on the grounds that the alcoholic may no longer force the spouse to live in an intolerable situation. In effect it is saying that the wife will not coerce the husband into sobriety, but she can no longer be forced to live under the intolerable drinking situation. It is giving the alcoholic the choice to drink, if this is more important than learning to stay sober and enter into the rebuilding of a marriage, with both parties seeking help in this process. For a wife who enters and remains in her own program, there is a reasonable chance of her working through grief regardless of the choice the alcoholic makes. She also has a real chance of motivating recovery for the alcoholic, with lasting sobriety, true reconciliation, and a good marriage being the possible results. Attempting to put a marriage back together without an alcoholism recovery program brings added grief for both persons.

There are additional losses for the spouse of an alcoholic husband as well as wife. The spouse may begin to suffer psychosomatic illness which interferes with work activities. Wives of drinking alcoholics may fail on the job in the same pattern that the alcoholic misses work. She has sick headaches, makes mistakes, and her absenteeism parallels the husband's stay at home. She may go to the doctor about her anxiety and grief related to alcoholism. Doctors see women in this condition more than they see husbands who are hungover. The wife also loses self-respect and is aware that she is not truthful with her doctor, covers up for her husband with his boss, and never tells the truth about her absenteeism with her own employer. This is the pattern of alcoholism. Grief is a normal reaction to the total aspects of alcoholism and therefore is something that can be understood, and plans can be made for working to overcome it.

Three Steps in Overcoming Grief

There are three basic steps in overcoming grief which may be taken by the grief-stricken person which do not require changing outside circumstances.

1. First one must make a sacrifice. This is true as related to death and other forms of grief. Despite the fact that all seems lost, the beginning of recovery requires the ability to give of one's self in a sacrificial manner. This is the first step out of the emptiness, the utter void of feeling that nothing is left. It is like overcoming paralysis by doing that which seems impossible. It requires faith and courage, but this is the beginning of conscious recovery. For the spouse of the alcoholic, it means giving up the "poor me" syndrome and doing something about the painful condition. It means going to Al-Anon meetings, or to group therapy, or both. It involves the help of other persons who understand and can join in the recovery process.

Essentially, it means an investment of time and energy in a sacrificial manner, in a program specifically designed to meet the needs of the spouse of the alcoholic which will permit her to overcome the sense of loss.

2. Secondly, it means giving up the three questions which begin with "why." "Why did I? Why did he? Why did we?" These questions are asked a million times by the spouse.

Or they can be asked in the negative form, "Why didn't I -- or he -- or we?" It is impossible in life to find an answer to "why" in human conduct, other than all persons exercise choice, and in the process of volition, people do what they want to do, and this is not always right or best for them or others. This is the way life is. There is no valid basis for the pursuit of "why," and in solving a problem, this is the first thing that must be abandoned.

The real problem cannot be faced until "why" is abandoned and one looks at "who, how, when, and where" things happened. Then and only then is it possible to decide what can be done about it from the point of view of changing one's self, one's attitude, and eventually, the reaction to what has happened. We cannot change what has happened. It has happened. It is a fact. We cannot change the historic fact, but we can change ourselves and our response to the fact.

In this aspect, basic religious truth must come into the picture. To ask "why" on a repeated basis is to blame God for letting it happen. If we take a good look at Biblical truth, we learn that God does not let us explain why we did things. We dare not make excuses in approaching God. The author of the Book of Job deals with the question of "why." Job cried out and asked God why all these things happened to him, a godly and upright man. The book deals with the suffering of one who is innocent and does not deserve all these losses. Finally, when Job understood he would be challenging God to continue the protest, he was able to change his whole approach and ask that God teach him. This is when Job began to heal and to be restored. It is the same process for all persons.

"Why" has to be abandoned in overcoming grief as well as in understanding the nature of one's own conduct. "Why" never appears in the creed of any religious faith and is certainly not in any form of confessional. Nor is it found in the Lord's

Prayer, Ten Commandments, the Serenity Prayer, nor the Twelve Steps of AA or other similar groups.

If we cannot tell God why we did anything other than it was our own human choice and that we are responsible for what we did, then we cannot demand that others tell us why. To do so would be assuming that we could push God aside and demand that persons answer to us in a way that God will not permit us in our relationship with Him. And like Job, we cannot find fault with God as Job did initially and demand that He tell us why things happened.

So "why, why, why?" has to go, and the focus must be placed on one's own healing.

3. The final step may be termed sanctification, which is the ability to see the lost person or object in an entirely different light. It is a releasing in love that which has been lost. If it is the death of a loved one, it is giving back to God with thanksgiving for the joy and happiness shared with the person before the loss. In alcoholism, it is releasing the alcoholic in love and seeing whatever is good in the alcoholic and being thankful for it without bitterness, anger, hatred, or resentment. It does not mean that one continues to be an unnecessary martyr to alcoholism. Sanctification comes only as a final stage in one's own recovery; it is not the beginning of it.

This ability to see the alcoholic in a new light is a powerful force in the healing process, for it removes the spouse as a provoked female in the merry-go-round aspect of drinking, reaction, response, and drinking again. The reaction of the spouse is now entirely different, so the response must be different. The spouse no longer helps keep the merry-go-round going, and in most cases, this will lead to recovery of the alcoholic as well.

By resolving her own grief, the spouse can now act in freedom, as the intense pain of grief is so reduced it no longer controls her life. This also has tremendous impact on the grief of the children, who also are freed by her freedom.

Children in a family with alcoholism suffer grief, for they lose not only their security with the alcoholic parent but also lose the other parent to alcoholism by the focus of the sober spouse on the alcoholic. It is not the drinking or drunkenness that cuts the children off, but the fighting and quarreling that does it. Also the children see both parents so involved with each other and the drinking problem that they are left out, and neither parent is seriously concerned with the needs of the children.

A case history will illustrate it. Recently, a forty-two-year-old wife in Al-Anon heard a lecture on grief as it relates to alcoholism, and two days later a program on reconciliation with one's family of origin as the basis of mental health. She put the two together and became aware of the fact that when she was fifteen, she felt that she lost her mother to her father's alcoholism. Later the father died, and she resolved this grief. However, twenty-seven years later there was still a painful relationship with her mother which she recognized as grief which had never been reconciled.

This woman learned she can turn back to her mother, work toward reconciliation with her and overcome the grief. Not only is it her responsibility to do this, but she is aware of the joy she will have in the reconciliation.

Working through grief and achieving sanctification is a problem for children of alcoholics who grow up. There are some who claim that the injury which occurs during the early years of a child's life with an alcoholic parent cannot be removed later on. For adults who still suffer grief from childhood experiences, it is never too late to overcome the grief reaction. Recovery from alcoholism is a lifelong process. For the alcoholic, the spouse, and their children, it does not occur in a thirty-day treatment program for the alcoholic.

How to Help

How does one help a grief-stricken person? There are some things which often prove beneficial and other things which may be avoided.

First and foremost, when a person is suffering from grief, your presence is helpful if you are a loved one and your presence is one of comfort. Most rush in at the first indication of grief and do not go back again when the real problem stretches out over a long period of time. Grief does not disappear quickly. In some cultures and families, when death occurs, other members of the extended family do not let a widow live alone at home for a year or more. A sister, aunt, cousin, or niece is scheduled by family planning to provide residential companionship of a loved one to help the mourning person through the grief period. So the two things you can always give a grieving person are your companionship and your love.

When visiting a grieving person, lend an ear and not a mouth. Do not advise and counsel as did Job's comforters. They tried to tell him why it all happened and nearly drove him out of his mind. Do not try to solve the problem, just be there. Do not try to make him eat, but see that food is available that can be eaten in small quantities. If the grieving person suggests an activity, join him, but do not push or insist that he do what you think he should do. Remaining in familiar surroundings is essential.

Remember also that healing is as much a part of life as sickness or hurt. Time is necessary in healing, but grief should not be prolonged. Overcoming grief is a spiritual process, and those who wish to participate in spiritual healing need to understand that in spiritual healing, one must be a wounded healer. If a person has not been through real grief, it is impossible to say that "I understand how the grieving person feels." If one has experienced grief, one knows that this need not be said. Your presence and your compassion indicate that you understand the need of the other person and that you really understand how he feels. Your presence conveys the message.

Al-Anon Is Helpful

For the spouse of an alcoholic or for other members of the family, there is one group that is capable of providing the healing process in overcoming grief. By the very nature of its program, Al-Anon provides this, as it is a program of spiritual recovery based on the same Twelve Steps and Traditions of Alcoholics Anonymous. The following are beneficial aspects of Al-Anon as they relate to grief, but there are many other benefits as well.

For the spouse or older children in a family where there is alcoholism, it becomes an extended foster family of caring persons who have been wounded and are healing. The fellowship of this group is one of understanding, and with this group support, the recovery from grief has increased assurance.

Also as the spouse learns to cope with alcoholism and makes basic changes, other members of her own family, especially the alcoholic, initially will often insist that she not rock the boat or that she turn back to where she was. He may even make threats if she does not return to the former position of riding the merry-go-round. If the spouse makes significant changes, she may find herself standing alone with all of the family, especially the in-laws, turned against her. Having an extended foster family at this time is essential in maintaining the recovery process.

This principle is the same as the fellowship of Alcoholics Anonymous when the alcoholic gives up his/her best friend, the bottle, and cuts off from his/her old drinking buddies, which is a basic part of recovery. Understanding persons are essential for the spouse, male or female, as well as for the alcoholic.

Using the Twelve Steps

The Twelve Steps are wonderfully structured for working through grief, and they are in complete accord with Biblical teaching and faith. First there is the process of surrender of self, which, in effect, is true sacrifice, admitting one is powerless and turning one's life over to the care of God. The other side of this coin is that one does not sit at home and do this. It means going out to the meetings. When God comes to us, he leads us to others with whom we can share our belief in restoration of faith. When we pray, we must put legs on our prayers by getting off our knees and doing something about the prayers we have just uttered. Admitting we are powerless over alcohol gives us the strength to do something about ourselves. At the same time, this is the abandonment of asking why and focusing on how the problem can be resolved.

The Fourth and Fifth Steps, taking one's own inventory and then making a complete confession to God and another human being, is a cleansing of guilt if complete honesty is followed in the inventory and confession. Once this has been accomplished, the loss can no longer be associated in any way as God's punishment for failures of the spouse, either of commission or ommission. It takes away from the spouse the feeling that drinking is her/his fault or that stopping it is her/his responsibility. Consciously or unconsciously, when the Fourth and Fifth Steps have been completed with honesty, it is impossible to blame God or one's self for the drinking and its consequences. It puts it where it belongs, the responsibility of the drinker, who may continue to drink in a destructive manner or enter a recovery program. It also helps the spouse understand that any statement on the part of the alcoholic as to why drinking occurs is an alibi and cannot be accepted.

In completing the Twelve Steps, the spouse achieves that state of condition which permits sanctification. By releasing the alcoholic in love, one gives back to God and to the alcoholic the responsibility of deciding what to do. It gives the spouse the freedom to remember what is good in the alcoholic and to remember the joy in the life shared with this person as well as the sorrow. This minimizes the loss.

In this process of releasing in love and permitting the alcoholic to choose to drink or seek help in learning to abstain, the spouse is not required to separate or is not required to remain in the marriage. This is the choice of the spouse, who knows not only what is best, but also what is possible for her/him to do at this particular time.

The new freedom of the spouse and the ability to cut the strings which the alcoholic has used to control the spouse as a puppet have profound effect. In a reasonable period of time, most alcoholics seek help and enter their own program. If they do not or will not do this, the spouse at any time may offer the alcoholic reasonable choices as a condition of continuing the marriage or separation. In fact, the spouse may do this to discover if remaining as housekeeper or husband permits the alcoholic to choose not to do anything about the problem.

Finally, it means loving a person enough to permit him/her to fail in dignity without our interference, control, rescue, or protection. This means that we trust the built-in structure of life itself and its corrective measures, which just might be more successful than those we have practiced in the past. It also means giving up the effort to impose one's will on another person while accepting the responsibility of surrendering one's own to God's will, not to the alcoholic's demands.

Within the family system, healing is as contagious as sickness. When one member of the family seeks help and overcomes grief and remains in that condition of healing without changing back to the old method of dealing with problems, it is predictable that in time others in the family will move toward a recovery also. The real hope of the spouse and children or parents in an alcoholism situation is that of seeking help in overcoming their sense of loss. This, in a sense, is abandoning the alcoholic, but it is done in love. The hope is that this removal of the pampering and protection routine will result in the free choice of the alcoholic to surrender and admit he is powerless over alcohol and enter a recovery program.

If the spouse is the husband and the alcoholic a wife, the needs of the husband and his specific program are even greater. His role as husband is so controlling that unless he is able to overcome his grief and stop asking his wife and God why it all happens, there is little chance of recovery for either partner in the marriage. His healing is the most powerful condition that an alcoholic wife can experience. Few wives fail to respond when a husband overcomes his Pride and his Grief, and humbly seeks help for himself while releasing his wife in love.

A result of overcoming grief is the willingness and effort to share the healing experience with other persons who also suffer grief, especially from alcoholism. The Twelfth Step indicates that the person who has been through a spiritual recovery tries to take this message to others. The message can be extended, understanding and compassion can be offered, but the witness one bears in the practice of these principles is the means whereby others are able to accept the message and practice it in their lives. Once the healing occurs and there is understanding of how it happened, one is aware of the fact that the main thing worth offering is simply sharing our presence and our love.

As grief is the common experience of all persons and therefore is a normal condition -- not a pathology or sickness -- then recovery is a normal process and falls within the realm of normal spiritual experience. As each of us is able to release in love that person or thing that we have lost, so do we receive the healing power of God's grace. Also as our wounds are healed, so do we become instruments of God's grace in reaching out to others with the message of our recovery and the willingness and need to share this with all others who mourn.

Dr. Hans Lowenbach states that ninety percent of persons thought to be suffering depression are actually experiencing acute grief and deserve the dignity of knowing they are not mentally ill.

This is especially true in the area of alcoholism. The spouse is not a neurotic person who needs a drunk husband or wife, but an average person who is also a victim of alcoholism and experiencing grief, not depression. To know this, to accept it, and to act upon it has tremendous power in solving the problems of alcoholism for the alcoholic and the spouse who initiates the action. Children also benefit by such action on the part of the sober parent.

Today no one needs to remain in grief due to alcoholism. There are counselors who understand and there are thousands of Al-Anon groups capable of assisting the spouse through the steps in overcoming grief.

These steps are simple but profound in effecting a recovery from grief:

1. The willingness to make a sacrifice.

2. Stop asking "why?" which is to imply that God is guilty and we are innocent.

3. Sanctification, that condition which permits remembering that which is good rather than dwelling on that which has been lost.

Everyone has a choice: to remain in grief or to overcome it with the help of those who bear the scars of the same wounds.